A SURVIVOR'S GUIDE TO PANIC ATTACKS

Bev Aisbett

Thorsons
An Imprint of HarperCollins*Publishers*

Thorsons
An Imprint of HarperCollins*Publishers*
77–85 Fulham Palace Road,
Hammersmith, London W6 8JB

First published in Australia in 1993 as *Living With **IT***
Reprinted in 1994 (twice), 1995, 1996
by HarperCollins*Publishers* Pty Limited
ACN 009 913 517
A member of the HarperCollins*Publishers* (Australia) Pty Limited Group
Thorsons edition 1998

1 3 5 7 9 10 8 6 4 2
© Bev Aisbett 1993

Bev Aisbett asserts the moral right to
be identified as the author of this work

A catalogue record for this book
is available from the British Library

ISBN 0 7225 3665 8

Printed and bound in Great Britain by
Woolnough Bookbinding Limited, Irthlingborough, Northamptonshire

Contents

Introduction

Dr D. Jefferys, Ph.D

Witnessing recovery from panic to a point where the sufferer is no longer fearful and dependent and functions enthusiastically with fulfilment in the world is a satisfying part of being a psychologist.

This book is written by a patient for patients from a patient's perspective, demystifying Panic Disorder, thus making it comprehensible to all. For the psychologist/counsellor, it provides insight into the fearfulness experienced by those who have panic disorder.

Panic disorder is characterised by the panic attack, the **'IT'** whose symptoms include palpitations, nausea, dizziness, light-headedness, a choking sensation, difficulties with breathing and perhaps most significantly, an elevated level of fearfulness and dread.

Advances in psychology and pharmacotherapy mean that a sufferer need suffer no more. With treatment, a patient is able to recover and enter the world armed with the knowledge which enables the individual to monitor, challenge and calm their own fear.

A Survivor's Guide to Panic Attacks is a ready guide of 'tools' that will assist the patient in dealing with panic and themselves in their everyday lives. It is a handbook, a workbook and a source of hope and affirmation.

A Survivor's Guide to Panic Attacks conveys this information in a simple, disarming and immediate form: the visual. I am pleased to have been involved (in an advisory capacity) in the development of this valuable aid. The fact of this book's existence is proof that full recovery is possible with the help of a therapist and through one's own endeavours.

Foreword

I first encountered my **'IT'** on a glorious blue day in Sydney, on what was meant to be a pleasant weekend visit to attend the Australian National Cartoonists' awards – the 'Stanleys'.

The sky was a flawless canopy, the yachts bobbed cheerily on the harbour, tourists snapped photos of smiling friends on the foreshore, and there I stood, struck dumb by the enormity of what I was experiencing.

Most people who suffer Panic Syndrome (and suffer is the word!) remember their first Panic Attack.

It is overwhelming, utterly terrifying and remains etched in the memory for a long time afterwards.

Hence a pattern develops, as this book shows.

In the months that followed this initial attack, I was to return again and again to sources of reassurance, support and understanding that would eventually steer me out of the troubled, turbulent waters of this illness and back into the real world.

In doing so, and, in line with my chosen profession, I decided to create a handbook that would provide a ready guide, in a *patient's* language, to those same sources of help that saw me through this debilitating ailment.

A Survivor's Guide to Panic Attacks is not intended to be a substitute for professional help. I am in no way qualified to provide that.

I am, however, qualified, as a survivor, to pass on to fellow sufferers the kind of information and practices that were of great assistance to me, and in a form that will, hopefully, convey this information quickly, simply and with gentle disarmament, i.e. the cartoon.

My message to all Panic People is this: I *know* how you feel, and you *will* be well again. The book is testimony to that.

To those of you who may believe that your **'IT'** is far more fearsome than mine: while this is no competition (and if it were, what a useless one!), let me assure you that my **'IT'** woke me every day to the same tears and tremors and terrors that you may be feeling right now.

My thanks is beyond measure to all those who stood by me and, in particular, to one stranger who, without question or dismay, came to the aid of this bewildered soul on an unfamiliar street one dark, dark night, so long ago.

To all of you, take heart. One day this will be a far-off memory.

Trust me.

Trust yourself.

Bev Aisbett

Dedicated to the memory of Jeffe Jeffari my guardian angel...
... And heartfelt thanks and acknowledgement for assistance to
Dr Don Jefferys

If you have picked up this book, then you are probably experiencing some very strange and frightening things…

DOES THIS LOOK FAMILIAR?

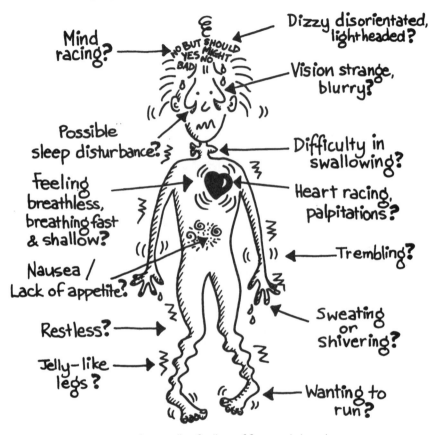

and overall, a feeling of fear and dread
that seems to come from nowhere?

Well, you have just joined
1000s of people who have **PANIC ATTACKS!***
* Also known as Panic Syndrome/Disorder,
or Anxiety Syndrome/Disorder

BUT... There is
GOOD NEWS!
→

GOOD NEWS SECTION

I.

At least 5% of the population has experienced
Panic Attacks and there may be many more people who,
for various reasons, keep their panic hidden. Others may not
experience actual panic, but suffer very
high levels of anxiety and unease.
With the right help, and in time, these people
can resume normal lives.

2.

YOU WILL NOT DIE

It may feel that way and, at times, you may even
have wished that you could. These are only feelings and
ideas. Both will pass. Many people believe
that they are having a heart attack instead of Panic
Attack, or that their heart cannot take the strain.
Remember, the heart is a tough muscle. It can cope.
After all, this is only **temporary.**

YOU WILL NOT GO MAD

What you are experiencing is a combination
of fearful thoughts and physical sensations,
usually arising after a period of stress.

AND –THE BEST NEWS OF ALL…

You **can** beat this!
You **will** get better!

HOW PANIC WORKS

It seems that out of a clear blue sky….

…you are suddenly struck by the most overwhelming sense of terror and dread imaginable.

Your first instinct is to run, to flee
from this agonising fear…

…You go into full Panic mode -
your heart races, you feel faint, you
shake, you sweat…

You can't imagine what could make you feel this terrible, so you search for a cause...

You decide you **must** be dying...

...or going crazy!...

...or that you will faint!

Eventually, when these sensations subside and you
find that nothing awful has happened to you,
you breathe a sigh of relief.

You have had your first PANIC ATTACK. You have met **'IT'**.

The trouble is, your brain
is now on the lookout
for **'IT'**.

Since you're still alive,
didn't faint and seem to be sane,
what could **'IT'** be?

Because you don't
know what **'IT'** is,

or where **'IT'** came from, you figure **'IT'** could sneak up on you again at *any* time,

and **'IT'** was so *horrible* you start to really worry...

You spend a lot of time wondering if or when **'IT'**
will strike again. You get *scared*. You get *tense*.

You become acutely aware of the slightest physical changes and
exaggerate them, believing they signal the
return of **'IT'**.

Your mind is on **RED ALERT**.
Your thoughts are racing.
It's like ten different radio stations
are tuned into your head.

By morning, you are
edgy and irritable…

…which makes you feel…

…guilty.

'SNAP OUT OF IT!'

you say (or someone else says).

'WHAT ON EARTH DO YOU HAVE
TO BE FRIGHTENED OF?'

The answer??
You're frightened of
'IT'.

WHAT IS 'IT'?

Let's start with what **'IT'** isn't.

'IT' is *not* an evil alien force.

'IT' is *not* spooks and demons.

'IT' is *not* Divine Punishment

OR...

... a sudden onset of insanityyy....

Hee Hee Hee

Heh Heh Heh

'IT' is *not* the work of a crazed ghoul who has tampered with the water supply.

AND...

'IT' does *not* come from watching too much television.

However, **'IT'** can feel *very* scary (this is to help your friends/family understand what you're feeling).

'IT' feels like you're in a crashing plane.

You feel unsafe in the world.

Everything that was once familiar and comforting now feels cold, alien and threatening.

Every minute is agony. You wonder how you will get through. You feel so *terrified*!

You cannot attach your fear to anything. There seems to be no *reason* for **'IT'**.

'IT' is this big, awful, hideous, scary thing that has turned your life upside down.

BUT!!

(this is for you now)

'IT' is your *own* physical sensations.
'IT' is your *own* fearful thoughts.
'IT' is *nothing more* than this.

Believe it or not, you helped to invent your **'IT'** *all by yourself!*

'IT' is *your* creation!

Recipe for an "IT"

(Serves none)

4 truckloads of guilt
16 cups of shoulds
4 bags of perfectionism
12 busloads of criticism (self or outside)
10 barrels of low self-esteem
20 tonnes of negative thoughts
80 kilos of exaggeration
1 football field worth of worrying
Large pinch of sense of failure
1 period of insomnia*

Combine with any of the following:

I major life change

I or more relationship problem(s)

I or more drug experience(s)

I prolonged period of tension

I set of gynaecological problems/hormonal changes

I inability to relax

I ridiculous work load

I unhappy childhood

I set of sexual problems

I family member with Panic Disorder or Anxiety Condition

I biological predisposition

Ingredients may vary with each individual

Allow mixture to simmer for most of a lifetime.

SO...

you have a *base* of negative thoughts…

to which you *add* a stressful situation…

followed by a *topping* of physical sensations…

AND...

Voila!

Your own, personal **IT**

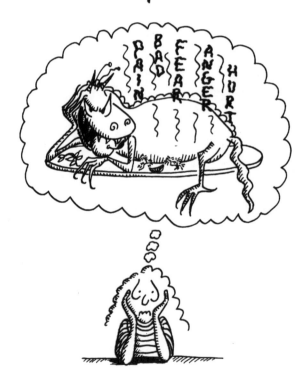

Quite a concoction!

Now that you've cooked up your **'IT'**
and **'IT'** has grown legs and free ranges around
your life making you utterly miserable, you need
to set down a few house rules.

The next section will show you how to begin…

HOUSETRAINING YOUR 'IT'

IT LITTER

Step 1:
ACCEPTANCE

Like him or not, your **'IT'** has
moved in: lock, stock and Panic Attack
That is the *present* reality.

It is difficult to accept this.
You don't want **'IT'**. You don't like **'IT'**.

In fact, you wouldn't wish **'IT'** on your worst enemy.

'No,' you think, 'there's been a mistake. **"IT"** is an exotic illness.' You have a check-up, just to prove it.

It's hard to live with **'IT'** let alone accept **'IT'**. You miss your old life, old self. You grieve for the person you *think* you've lost forever.

It's not fair! **'IT'** is not fair! You want **'IT'** gone. NOW!

You want your life back! How *dare* **'IT'** do this to you!
Go AWAY!

Guess what? He's still there.

WHY?

Because **'IT'** is shaped by **you** and **your** thoughts.
So, stop wishing and grieving and rebelling and denying.
Giving in does not mean giving up.
After all, **'IT'** is *anxiety*, nothing more than that!

Yes, he <u>is</u> **BIG** and **UGLY** and **TERRIFYING**

But <u>**YOU**</u> designed him!

Acceptance does not mean that you have to *love* **'IT'**
or even *like* **'IT'**. In fact, right now, you *hate* **'IT'**.

Acceptance is somewhere in between such strong
emotions in a calm, central, neutral place.

You have **'IT'**, **'IT'** is unpleasant, but that's how **'IT'** is.
You *have* **'IT'**, in the same way as you *have* a bad
headache or you *have* a strong emotion.

It's the same as living with diabetes, for instance. Let **'IT'** roll.
'IT' is just something you live with…
FOR NOW.

Step 2:
BREATHING

'IT' is in full flight. He's having a field day. This is what you do:

STOP  for a few seconds and observe your breathing. It is probably shallow, quick, and high up in your chest. You may be doing an awful lot of sighing

 or panting.

You are letting off too much carbon dioxide (CO_2).
You are **hyperventilating** and this makes you
feel weird and agitated.

NOW – without lifting
your shoulders, place your
hand on your abdomen
and take a big, s-l-o-w
breath till your abdomen
expands. Hold it in.

Think *only* of your breathing.
It is the *most important* thing right now.

Now, let *all* the air out, very slowly,
till your abdomen goes *in* again.
KEEP GOING
slowly, in … and … out, in … and … out.

'IT' is confused by this.

He thinks: 'Hang on, you're supposed to be *scared* and
you're *relaxing*!!! You're *ignoring* me!!!'

Yes, you *are* ignoring **'IT'**. Breathing is the important
thing right now. You are busy restoring your CO_2 level
to normal. Keep going…in and out, in and out.
This is *your* time. You can breathe anywhere,
any time that **'IT'** decides to bite.

For added ammunition, find a comfortable,
quiet place to lie down.

Put on some soothing music or a relaxation
tape and continue with your breathing.
'IT' may hang around for a while, but he *hates*
this New Age stuff and he *hates* being ignored.

He'll head off and sulk.

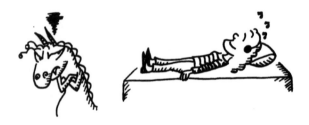

He's persistent, though, so you must be, too. More so.
Do this as often as you need to.

Step 3:
FLOATING PAST

In you mind, cast away your trembling, snarling,
biting **'IT'** on an island.

You are safely drifting past in a small boat.

'IT' is raging and roaring, but you are in your boat and
all you feel is distant ripples. This is not your concern
because you are just an observer, passively watching.
Let **'IT'** roar all **'IT'** likes. Remember, **'IT'** is just a
Panic Attack, nothing more sinister than that.

Step 4:
WAITING 'IT' OUT

In the early stages of your life with **'IT'**,
the pain may seem to be endless and
always at an unbearable level.
'IT' is with you day after day,
and the claw of fear in your stomach
is *almost* constant.

ALMOST…but not totally.
In fact, even a formidable force
like **'IT'** gets tired from pummelling
you after a time.

If you were to make a graph, you would find that the panic is not really
constant, nor is it always at its highest pitch.

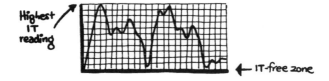

There are even some **'IT'** – free periods in between!

Try charting your levels of panic on a scale of 1 to 10
and see how they actually fluctuate. **'IT'** is not
always full-on. By deep breathing and floating, it is possible
to wait for the worse moments to pass.
They always do.
Focus on that fact. Make it a chant.

Interestingly, if you were to *will* yourself to panic, you probably wouldn't. It is your *fear* of panic that makes it happen.

Return to Steps 1 to 4 as often as you need to.
They will help you to accept that **'IT'** need not overwhelm you. You *can* control **'IT'**!

WELL DONE!

Now, move on.

'WALKIES' WITH 'IT'

The first thing you are tempted to do in your
co-habitation with **'IT'** is to do nothing!
'IT' demands so much of your time, energy and attention,
you feel you cannot take on *one more thing*.

'IT' makes you feel so overwhelmed, it is hard to concentrate, or
make a decision or perform the simplest task.
He is in your head constantly, whispering poisonous ideas.
It's hard to think straight.

Eventually, you spend all your time thinking of **'IT'**.
This feeds him so he grows and grows till you cannot
function any more. **'IT'** has pinned you down.

Perhaps your home is actually **'IT'** free.
Perhaps you left him in the supermarket in Aisle 3
next to the pet food, where you first found him.
Too bad you now have to do without pet food!

Or, you may have left him on a plane, whizzing
around to all the places *you* would like to go!

Or, **'IT'** may be as close as your own front gate.

'IT' may make you afraid of crowds or people or trains
or dogs or roads or music or trees or life or death
or wars or a television show or pollution or friends or…

In fact, the list can be endless.
Anything you associate with **'IT'** can make
you panic again.

STOP!

Think for a minute. **'IT'** is yours, remember…

…and **you** are allowing *your* **'IT'** to hold you prisoner!

It's not the supermarket that's scary. It's just a supermarket. Your *thoughts* about the supermarket are what is scaring you.

No matter what you are afraid of, be it

or

in some way **'IT'** is preventing you from enjoying *your* life!

'IT' goes hand in hand with phobias.
Phobias are **'IT's** tools of trade.

The most common phobias
associated with Panic Attacks are:
AGORAPHOBIA
(a fear of open spaces) and
CLAUSTROPHOBIA
(a fear of closed spaces).

A phobia develops because you link being afraid with being in a certain place or situation. However, being afraid has little to do with the actual setting, but rather what you were *thinking* about and how you *felt* in that setting.

Say you had a Panic Attack in a crowded lift. You were probably thinking:
'What if it gets stuck?'
'What if I can't get out?'
'We'll run out of air and I won't be able to breathe.'

Then, as a result of these thoughts, your breathing *does* become more shallow, your heart beats faster and you feel as though you are suffocating. Suddenly, you are desperate to get out.

There is an added ingredient here, too. The lift is crowded.

 There are strangers all around you who will see you lose **control**! This adds to your anxiety. So, you panic.

From here on, you swear you will NEVER set foot in a lift again. You develop a phobia. You believe you can regain control by *avoiding* the situation in which you were afraid.

But avoidance actually means *loss* of control.

Lifts are out for a start,

 then trains because they're confined too,

 and planes,

 and eventually any small space.

Control comes from *rethinking* the situation.
Control means acknowledging that the lift did open,
that you did *not* suffocate, that most if not all of your
fellow passengers did *not* notice that you were afraid,
and that lifts are generally safe.

It was *your* **thoughts** that made you afraid.

Ask yourself: What's the worst thing that **'IT'** could do to me?

DID THEY?

Well... I don't know... one lady helped me ...

SEE?

But **IT** could ruin my life!

OH HOW??

Well, I get so scared I can't do anything!

WHAT ARE YOU SCARED OF?

'IT'!!

AND WHAT IS 'IT'?

Um... well...
my own creation...
...um, fear...

SO ALL YOU ARE AFRAID OF IS...

Well...
yes!

BEING AFRAID!

HOW TO BEGIN

When **'IT'** is roaring and raging, inactivity will keep
you focused only on how bad you feel.
This can create a vicious cycle.

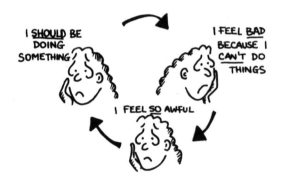

Ask yourself: What can I achieve if I act?

A. If I need to concentrate on something, I can't concentrate on **'IT'**.

B. I could feel better about myself.

C. I could feel a sense of purpose.

D. I could feel I have regained some control.

SO... Make a start. Right now. Begin to *reclaim* **your** life.

START SMALL AND BUILD UP, EACH DAY.

Try making a list:

Remember – if you are going into **'IT'** overload, *breathe*.
Tell yourself: 'This will pass.' Don't stop what
you're doing! Keep going! Focus on each task, not on how
you're feeling. Each task is **important**.

Doing these things means that you are working to
resume **your** life. You are taking back the reins.
It helps if you concentrate on what you're doing.
For instance, when you ring Susie, try not to mention
how you're feeling. Shift the focus.

Listen to what Susie is saying.
Ask questions. If Susie asks
you how you're feeling,
tell her the truth. You're

trying not to think about that at the moment.
You're taking time out. You may need to talk about
'IT' but not right now.

As you complete each item on the list, tick them off.

Congratulate yourself.
Each completed activity is an achievement.

You did not **DIE** or even **FAINT!**

Nothing **HORRIBLE**
happened to you!

You were still able to do things…

Despite feeling scared!!

Therefore…

feels scared, but
does things
= things done
despite feeling
scared
= things done
anyway!

FEELING
SCARED
IS
NOT
IMPORTANT

Believe it or not, one day you will be doing something and you'll realise you've **forgotten** to be scared!

Eventually…

THE
PHYSICAL
'IT'

One of the reasons why **'IT'** keeps popping up is that your mind confuses natural **physical** changes – especially **stress** reactions – with the first signs of impending **Panic Attack.**

GRUMP
GRUMP

ABOUT STRESS

As humans, we first learned about stress when our survival depended on it.

If a dinosaur in a bad mood happened to cross your path, your mind would flash signals to alert your body to act in your own best interests.

Your body was prepared for 'flight' (fleeing) or fight – to act in response to danger.

There may be no more dinosaurs, but our response to outside stressors remains the same.

The heart rate increases, pumping blood into the muscles, the stomach tightens to move blood toward the extremities, you sweat to cool the skin and there is a rush of adrenalin, which causes shaking.

Stress reactions can also be triggered by pleasant sensations, such as anticipation, excitement, sexual arousal or exercise.

So – these feelings are neither good nor bad, but the way we **perceive** them is subject to the situations we **associate** them with.

Stress reactions occur with:

EXERTION

ANXIETY

and

EXCITEMENT

At the start of this book, you saw the range of symptoms associated with Panic Syndrome.

All of these reactions occur because we **perceive** danger and our bodies get prepared to take on the dinosaur, the **'IT'**. However, a Panic Attack is a false alarm. There is no external threat, so a vicious cycle begins. Even a mild physical change, or reaction to stress, can set up this cycle.

FALSE!!
ALARM..

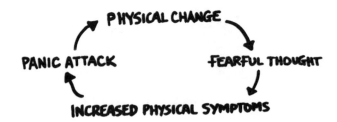

YOU ARE AFRAID OF BEING AFRAID
AND THE FIRST SIGN OF FEAR IS –

PHYSICAL SENSATION!

A whole range of things can set off physical changes
and stress reactions.

Normally, you might not even notice them, but (remember?) you are
on **'IT'** alert at the moment, so they can become distorted or
misinterpreted in your mind.

Some of these triggers are:

Caffeine

Fatigue

Hunger

Alcohol

Strenuous Activity

Watching suspenseful or violent images

Hormonal Changes (Menstruation, PMS, Menopause)

Intense emotion

AND THEN...

…there are the usual daily stressors of work and relationships and deadlines, and traffic jams…

SO…

you need to learn to differentiate between everyday stress and Panic Attacks. You need to recognise physical sensations for what they are – **PHYSICAL.**

There is no need to bring **'IT'** on to the scene at all.

Say to yourself…

This is just my body's response to stress.
There is no outside danger.

Don't add fearful thoughts and the vicious cycle stops
RIGHT HERE!

THE
THINKING
'IT'
OWNER

CHECKLIST FOR AN **'IT'** OWNER

Not everyone qualifies to own an **'IT'**.
You need to be a special kind of thinker. **Try this checklist:**

I worry a lot over things that might not happen ❑
I tend to exaggerate ❑
I expect to be able to deal with *anything* ❑
I strive for perfection ❑
I feel that, when compared to others, I am lacking ❑
I expect to be liked by and to like *everyone* ❑
I am often accused of being over-emotional ❑
I am not happy with my appearance most of the time ❑
I tend to push myself too hard ❑
I do not 'suffer fools gladly' ❑
I tend not to make time to relax ❑
I find my emotions spill over easily ❑

or

I have difficulty in showing my emotions ❑

I spend a lot of time thinking about old hurts,
    injustices and regrets ❑

I worry about what people think of me ❑

I feel uneasy/scared if I cannot control a situation ❑

I tend to criticise others and myself ❑

I often find myself thinking 'I should' or 'I wish' or 'What if' ❑

I have trouble 'letting go' of a situation ❑

I always have to be right ❑

'IT' owners are great thinkers. They do lots of it, and lots of it is negative, otherwise they wouldn't own an **'IT'**!

Remember the recipe? Ingredients like criticism, guilt, worry, negativity…that's your **'IT'**.

So it's time to see this monster for what he really is…

A NAG

'IT' is that poisonous voice in your head, telling you over and over that you blew this, or messed up that, or that you're not good enough, or that you're foolish, too fat, too thin, too weak, too stupid, that you're *always* this or *never* that, that you *should* be better, but you *can't* do anything, you're hopeless, incompetent, ugly, lazy, petulant, bad, over-emotional, pathetic…on and on and on, nag, nag, nag, day in, day out.

He's even started to brag about himself lately, hasn't he? He says…

'IT' has a whole list of thought patterns to use on
you and bring you down…

Here are the main ones…

1.EITHER-OR

You see one bad situation as the permanent situation. Either you're **dazzling** this time, or you never were!

2.BLAME-ME

Everything is *your* fault and *your* responsibility: the weather, the behaviour of your guests, your company's bankruptcy, your spouse's cooking.If there's a problem - you caused it!

3.ONE GOOF-TOTAL GOOF!

One mistake and that's it. You'll *never* be any good, you *always* mess up! *No one* makes as many mistakes as you!

4.BAD-TAGS

A whole dictionary of clichés and put-downs that bundles everyone into little sealed, tagged boxes. Used widely by fascists, idiots and wimps (see??)

5. SELECTIVE MEMORY

Whoops! What colour are those glasses? Certainly
not rose! Did you tell your friend about the great cruise,
the friendly service, the beautiful scenery and the night
you danced on the tables with 25 new friends?
Somehow, you forgot that.

6. ME, ME, ME

Uh oh. The whole universe centres around you. *You* are being judged and observed for faults all the time.

You enter a room. Either *everyone* is *staring* at you or *everyone* is *ignoring* you. (P. S. They're not!)

7. CLAIRVOYANCE

Oh, the pitfalls of amateur telepathy! And you just know that facial flicker on the other person means bad news for you! How could they be thinking anything good about you?

8. THE SKY IS FALLING!

Chicken Licken was probably the first to introduce total freak-out into folklore, but **'IT'** owners make it an art form. Your mind leaps from one (surmountable) problem through a whole series of spin-offs that have you arriving at total annihilation!

... and so on!

This is just a sample of those **'IT'** whispers that pull you down, day after day, year after year. No wonder you're feeling bad!

WHAT POISON!

What a bore! What a drag!
What a bundle of dead weight to heave around!
Where does he get this stuff from, anyway?

Notice how there are no grey
areas in **'IT'** statements.
They are inflexible absolutes:
**everything, always, everybody,
no one, never, nothing, ever,
total, complete.**

Then there are his weapon words:
can't, won't, might, must, ought and, nastiest of all: **should.**

And **'IT'** is so sure. **'IT'** just **knows.**

HOW
Does IT know?

Not exactly a reliable source, is **'IT'**, really?

Optimism??
Yuk!

Has it ever occurred to you that **'IT'**
never has anything **GOOD** to say???

FACING 'IT'

If someone subjected your best friend to the kind of punishment that **'IT'** doles out to you, surely you would intervene.

You would **defend** them.

You would seek out further **evidence** before making final **judgements**.

You would not encourage **ugly gossip** about them.

You would appreciate their **individuality**…

…and accept that, at times they have views that do not fit others' ideals.

You would **forgive** them their mistakes…

You would **support** them…

You would **help** them to
find **solutions** to their
problems…

and you would not **expect**
the **impossible** from them.

In other words...

YOU'RE A GOOD FRIEND!

To everyone, that is, except **yourself.**
Perhaps you need to change your **thinking.**

Your thoughts have a profound effect on the way you feel and if these thoughts are mainly negative, your feelings about yourself and the world will be equally bleak. If you tell yourself the worst, then you expect it and usually get it.

But – your thoughts can be changed, simply because you **learned** to think that way in the first place! It's a matter of **re-educating** yourself to think differently. Listen in: what are you **telling** yourself?

STEPS TOWARDS CHANGING YOUR THINKING

Let's do a bit of talking back to **'IT'**! He's held the floor for ages, now, **unchallenged.** Now it's your turn. Let's start with Panic Attacks.

STEP 1. Challenge negative thoughts

Ask yourself if the negative statement is actually true, or whether it is an exaggeration or distortion.

STEP 2. Demand evidence

What is the idea based on? What are the facts?

STEP 3. Reason it out

Ask yourself what the most likely outcome of a situation could be?

STEP 4. Substitute with a better option

Give yourself an alternative to the worst-case scenario. There are always options.

STEP 5. Scrap 'shoulds'

Should is a very damaging word. It hems you in.
It punishes you. Try using **could** instead.

STEP 6. Allow yourself to feel good

If it happens that you catch yourself feeling good, indulge yourself. Give
yourself permission. Don't self-sabotage.

GO ON – BE A FRIEND – TO YOURSELF.
(Would it hurt?)

THINKING, NOT PANICKING

You will need to do a bit of work on your thinking
even when **'IT'** is off dozing somewhere.
As we saw earlier in this section, there are a lot of
nasty whispers in your head that have helped to
create your **'IT'** in the first place.

TRY THESE TACTICS...

Ask: 'Do I really have enough
evidence to reach a conclusion?

Leave the **predictions** to the
soothsayers!

Hey! No **name-calling**, OK?

If something doesn't go to
plan…Will it be

LOOK for the positive option!

There **are** alternatives.

REMEMBER:
No **one** and no **thing** can **make** you feel a certain way. You govern your feelings.

HOWEVER –

We all have
good days…

…and ~~bad~~
not-so-good days.

It's all just part of the

**RICH
TAPESTRY
OF LIFE!**
(P.S. Learn to love clichés)

Feeling LOUSY?

Maybe it's not **cancer** or a **brain tumour** or something **terminal** after all! Maybe you're tired.

Does it really matter what most people **think** of you?

Avoid comparing yourself to others.

...but you are **not** the **centre of the universe!**

Sometimes...

...some things just
can't be helped.

PAT
PAT

Acknowledge your
achievements!

WHIP
WHIP
WHIP

Be realistic about getting things done.
Find a **balance**. **Pace** yourself.

After all...Is the **dead**line
a **life** or **death** line?

And, for
failing
to meet
the deadline...

Do you like **every**body?

Does **every**body
have to like you?

I just wanted to thank you for being patient. I haven't been very well lately.

HOWEVER...

it's a good idea not to
jump to conclusions!

Look! Up in the sky!

I don't see anything!

AND LASTLY...
(but not least!)
You are not
SUPER PERSON

Have you noticed something?
'IT' is not **quite** as powerful as he was.

Even if you've only just begun, even if you notice only the slightest shift, you have already made progress.

You have started to reclaim your life.

BE PATIENT with yourself. You are

learning a great deal about yourself. It takes time to adjust. It takes time to heal. You will need to be **COMMITTED** to progress. **'IT'** hates being challenged. He thrives on doom and gloom and hopelessness. He loves lies, mistruths and distortions.

Stop feeding him these and **in time** he'll stop gnawing at **you.**

HERE'S A MIRROR

TAKE A LOOK

You **deserve** to be happy. You're actually nice!

You try hard, you mean well.

You do the best you can , given your circumstances.

You do what is appropriate for you, at this time.

Memorise this ➡️

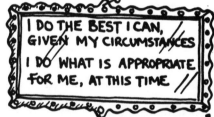

I DO THE BEST I CAN, GIVEN MY CIRCUMSTANCES

I DO WHAT IS APPROPRIATE FOR ME, AT THIS TIME

It applies to EVERYONE!

TRY THIS: Observe the differences in others and yourself without judgement for just one day.

No labels, no categories, no put-downs, no name-calling.

It's very liberating to do this. Why? Because the pressure's off.

- You no longer have to **compete** with or **impress** those you **believe** are superior.

- You no longer have to **compare** yourself to others.

- You no longer have to feel frustrated or angry with others because you are **impartial**.

- You no longer need to feel that some people are out of bounds because they are **better** or **worse** than you.

You just *are*. They just *are*.

You and they have had to find unique ways to survive.

If you can do this exercise for one day, why not try it all the time? It's powerful. It's a relief.

So as a final stunning tactic…Give everybody (including yourself) a holiday!

NON – 'IT' OWNERS

This is about the people you encounter; the people you live with, be they family, friends, colleagues or strangers.

They may say…

These responses can leave you feeling worse. You feel *misunderstood* or that your pain has been *trivialised*, or you feel *guilty* for feeling bad for no (apparent) reason.

But then again - there will be people who say…

OR

OR

All these people are reacting in ways that are **appropriate to them at the time** (remember?).

They are reacting in response to several factors.

These include:

- Their own experience
- Their own personality
- Their own level of understanding
- Their own ability to empathise
- Their own ability to express their feelings
- Their own problems
- Their own ability to cope
- Their own set of beliefs

There will be some people who are able to help you more than others. Don't be afraid to ask for that help and don't worry about the rest.

However – especially with family and friends, it is important to remember that **'IT'** may be impacting on them almost as much as it is on you.

This should not add to your **guilt**, but simply be something to recognise when you can, and you may need to make some allowances for others who are going through this with you.

They, too, may be **TIRED**...

Hi dear, I'm home!

...or **FRUSTRATED**

...or they may feel **HELPLESS**

...or even **ANGRY**

This doesn't mean they love you less.

Often they simply do not know what to do.

HERE'S WHAT THEY CAN DO

(show them this)

1. Listen

Panic People need to let it out. Often.
Panic People need to talk it through. Often.

2. Encourage

Recognising that the Panic Person is trying will spur them on.
Encourage them to keep going, but never bully them or become
impatient. They are doing their best. They need your support.

3.Be the voice of reason

If the Panic Person is feeling chaotic, step in and guide them back to a point of focus. Encourage them to *think* rather than let their feelings run away with them. *Reason* it out together.

4.Understand that this is very real to the Panic Person. There may be very severe physical symptoms.

5.Avoid Surprises

The Panic Person needs to pace him/herself. They may need to plan ahead, so they can deal with each new situation.

6. Acknowledge each achievement

However small it may seem, to the Panic Person completing a new task may have meant climbing a mountain. Remind them, too, of their progress. They may forget at times.

7. Try to be patient

This is hard, but getting angry or showing frustration will only make the Panic Person feel guilty. It takes time and effort to change, and remember, you are well; you have more reserves to call on.

8. Become informed

It is a great help if you know about the strategies that will help the person through to recovery. You can then work with them to achieve their goal and return **both** your lives to normal.

You, the Panic Person, can also help your family and friends by telling them what **you** need them to do if you're panicking.

OWNING
YOUR
'IT'

You have probably asked the following questions many times:

Question I.

WHY ME??

Why is this awful, bad, hideous
thing happening to me?

There are basic problems with this line of thinking.
The very question Why me? suggests that **'IT'** comes
from the outside, as if you have been selected in a giant
cosmic lottery and your **'IT'** has been allotted to you.

This concept can work against you in several ways.

By believing that **'IT'** has been imposed on you, you give **'IT'** control. You become a victim, waiting to be rescued.

In this situation, **'IT'** can take on many guises.

'IT' can be other people who make you feel uneasy.

'IT' can be places that make you feel scared.

Or **'IT'** can appear in situations that make you feel uncomfortable.

Did you spot the major flaw in the above statements?
Nothing can **make** you feel a certain way. No **one** can
make you feel a certain way. Your feelings belong to **you.**

It's the same with **'IT'**. When you see **'IT'** as something
that *happens* to you, outside of your control, you give **'IT'**
absolute power over your life.

Off with her head!

Question 2.

WHAT HAVE I DONE TO DESERVE THIS?

This suggests you are being punished.
But by whom? For what?

You are **not being punished.**
You are not **bad.** You are not **wrong.** Your
thinking has become a bit wonky, that's all.

Try to observe your thinking in everyday situations:
Let's say you've had a bad day – (everybody has them).

1. You oversleep
and are late for work…

Do you say:

2. You lose an important file. Do you say:

3. Your car breaks down. Do you say:

In each of these examples, you have the *choice* to either externalise the situation and apportion blame (it's the clock's, your boss's someone's, Alex's fault), or accept the situation and try to rectify it.

The same goes for **'IT'**.
Fighting **'IT'**, blaming **'IT'**, wringing your hands about **'IT'**, worrying about **'IT'** only gives **'IT'** power over you.
As long as you see yourself as a victim, you remain powerless.

YOU'RE THE BOSS!

Question 3

BUT HOW DID I GET 'IT' IN THE FIRST PLACE?

It's natural to want to find a cause, something to pin these awful feelings on. But we are complex beings and the causes may also be complex, numerous and hidden. Ask yourself: if you knew right now that the reason you have **'IT'** is that you nearly drowned as a child (for instance), would that make **'IT'** totally disappear?

Probably not, because you have developed a pattern of thinking about your anxiety that needs to be adjusted in the here and now.

Think of all the energy and attention you are giving to **'IT'**, for instance.

When you are anxious, you see every experience, every sensation, every encounter, every situation only in terms of **'IT'**'s effect on you.

Focusing on a cause may only add to your anxiety because, again, you are making pain the centre of your attention.

Get on with getting better.

There will be time to delve into the whys and
wherefores later, if you wish, and you will then be able to
follow your search from a position of **strength**.

By dealing with your immediate situation, and staying
in the here and now,

you are *empowering* yourself to **learn** from the past
and to **explore the possibilities** of the future.

RECRUITING AN 'IT' OBEDIENCE INSTRUCTOR

Your particular **'IT'** may be a bit too much of a handful to take on all by yourself at first. He may be keeping you up at all hours, demanding your attention.

His favourite trick is to stand on your chest so that you can't breathe properly, or to make your heart race or to confuse you into thinking that you're stuck with him forever! You're probably exhausted.

SO – CALL IN THE TROOPS!

A good counsellor will help with the house training of your **'IT'**, by guiding you through the steps towards recovery and by helping you to recognise areas of stress in your life and the way you deal with them.

He/she will also assist you in finding your own solutions to problems that might be causing conflict or unhappiness in your life and he/she will work with you to help in modifying patterns of thinking or behaviour that may be holding you back.

A good counsellor will serve as a confidante and friend, so chose someone that you feel very comfortable with. A counsellor may suggest drugs in the early stages of your **'IT'** encounter. Whether you take them or not is entirely *your* decision but, if your symptoms are particularly severe or debilitating, drugs may be a way for you to get some rest, and thereby regain strength and some space to get **'IT'** into perspective.

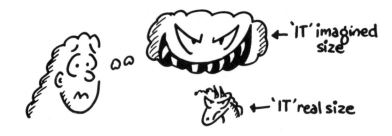

'IT' imagined size

←'IT' real size

You may be concerned about becoming addicted to the drugs and, if so, ensure that you discuss the proposed medication thoroughly with your counsellor and/or GP.

Remember: it's *your* choice.

It may be worth noting, however, that the kind of thinking that leads to addictive behaviour may be the very thinking that, with a counsellor's help, you are attempting to change. By the time you are ready to come off the drugs, you will have learned a great deal.

Most importantly, you will have someone to talk to who understands how you feel, and who will be able to actively assist you in returning to your normal life.

IT'S BACK

SETBACKS

Just when you thought it was safe…

Oh not again! It's the return of **'IT'**!

Well, he's persistent. He's had *years* of practice.

O.K. THINK about it!!

IMPORTANT POINT!

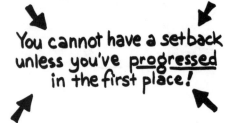

You cannot have a setback unless you've <u>progressed</u> in the first place!

SO – HAVING SETBACKS MEANS YOU'RE GETTING BETTER!

You are *not* at **BASE** I because you've already been there, done that!

You're stronger now, because you're better informed.
You know what to do. Keep going!

HERE ARE SOME REMINDERS:
Thousands of people
have overcome Panic. You can too.

Each time you feel anxious,
use correct breathing…

You are only **AFRAID** of the **FEAR** !

AND… Hop in your boat and **FLOAT** past the pain.

TUNE INTO YOUR THINKING →

1. Challenge.
2. Demand evidence.
3. Reason it out.
4. Supply a better option.

Are you back to old habits?

Remember – feeling scared is not IMPORTANT! Keep doing things! Keep busy!

KATHUMP! KATHUMP!

Are you confusing **FEAR** with **PHYSICAL SENSATIONS?**

MAKE FRIENDS WITH YOURSELF.

Acknowledge all that you've achieved!

Setbacks are part of the journey towards full recovery. It is not a matter of being in full Panic mode one day, then not the next. Recovery is gradual, a building process. This is because you have to relearn many things, and one is how to desensitise yourself to situations, sensations and locations that you would normally associate with being afraid.

This takes practice and exposure, till finally you are able to separate *places* from *Panic*, *feelings* from *Panic* and *ideas* from *Panic*.

But with every step, you remove yourself further and further from those first difficult days with **'IT'**.

Focus on your **progress** and not on your **pain**.
Be **committed** to **wellness**, not **illness**.

Assess what you are doing right now.
Are you working too hard? Can you pace it better?
Is something bothering you that can be changed?
Have you encountered a situation you find difficult to
handle? Can you ask for help?

This is temporary. This will pass.

YOU **WILL** BE ALL RIGHT!

A FINAL WORD

It's hard to see right now, but you have been presented
with an opportunity...

TO FEEL BETTER ABOUT YOURSELF
TO FEEL BETTER ABOUT OTHERS
TO FEEL BETTER ABOUT LIFE

You are learning how to be kinder to yourself.
You are learning how old habits held you back.
You are learning about patience.
You are learning acceptance.
You are learning tolerance.

AND...You are learning to focus on the things
that will help you progress, not just now, but throughout
your whole life. That has to rub off, doesn't it?

Maybe meeting **'IT'** was not a *completely*
bad thing, after all!

If you change the way you feel about **YOURSELF**, then you may
change the way you see **'IT'**. After all,
'IT' is you and you are **'IT'**

You might never find him *totally* loveable…

...but at least you can make peace.

AFTER ALL...

I know a **SURVIVOR** when I see one!